DATE DUE

CHICO MENDES

Fight for the Forest

GUYANA

SURINAME

FRENCH GUIANA

VENEZUELA

COLOMBIA

Amazon River

Trans-Amazon Highway

ECUADOR

AMAZÔNIA

Acre

BRAZIL

PERU

Brasília

BOLIVIA

PARAGUAY

CHILE

PACIFIC OCEAN

URUGUAY

ARGENTINA

ATLANTIC OCEAN

SOUTH AMERICA

CHICO MENDES

Fight for the Forest

Susan DeStefano
Illustrated by Larry Raymond

Twenty-First Century Books

A Division of Henry Holt and Co., Inc.

Frederick, Maryland

Published by
Twenty-First Century Books
A Division of Henry Holt and Co., Inc.
38 South Market Street
Frederick, Maryland 21701

Text Copyright © 1992
Susan DeStefano

Illustrations Copyright © 1992
Twenty-First Century Books

Printed in the United States of America

10 9 8 7 6 5 4 3 2 1

Library of Congress Cataloging in Publication Data

DeStefano, Susan
Chico Mendes: Fight for the Forest
Illustrated by Larry Raymond

(An Earth Keepers Book)
Includes glossary and index.
Summary: Relates the story of the rubber tapper who was murdered because
of his protest movement to stop the destruction of the Amazon rain forest.
1. Mendes, Chico, d. 1988—Juvenile literature.
2. Conservationists—Brazil—Biography—Juvenile literature.
3. Rubber tappers—Brazil—Biography—Juvenile literature.
4. Rain forest conservation—Brazil—Juvenile literature.
5. Rain forest conservation—Amazon River Region—Juvenile literature.
6. Deforestation—Brazil—Juvenile literature.
7. Deforestation—Amazon River Region—Juvenile literature.
[1. Mendes, Chico, d. 1988. 2. Conservationists.
3. Rain forest conservation—Amazon River Region.]
I. Raymond, Larry, ill. II. Title. III. Series: Earth Keepers
SD411.52.M46D47 1991
333.95′16′0981092—dc20 [B] 91-19734 CIP AC
ISBN 0-941477-41-X

CONTENTS

*"I have come to realize that what we
are fighting for is all of humanity."*

Chapter 1

The Signs of Struggle

Late in the summer of 1986, a group of men, women, and children made their way across a broad stretch of pasture. The pasture was part of a cattle ranch located in a faraway corner of western Brazil, in the heart of the Amazon rain forest.

In this part of the forest, the trees had been cut and burned to provide pastureland for cattle. The earth, once brimming with life, was now covered by a thin, scruffy layer of sun-bleached grass.

This drab pastureland was unlike the surrounding rain forest, where centuries of rain and sunshine had produced a dense, dark jungle. The constant chirping of birds and insects, hidden within the leaves of the forest, filled the air. A deep green canopy of trees and plants sheltered the forest floor like an umbrella. Not even the South American sun could pierce the lush foliage.

8

Now, as the group walked along, there were no trees to shield them from the scorching sun. There were no birds or insects to entertain them with noisy jungle songs. The only sounds were the soft murmurs of the people as they stepped across the ruined land.

Leading the group was a short, stocky man with a plump belly and a friendly face framed by thick, dark wavy hair. Wisps of curls lifted up around his neck and trimmed his forehead. His large, deep brown eyes seemed to reflect a calm, peaceful nature. The lines beneath his eyes crinkled whenever he smiled. Chico Mendes smiled often, turning up the corners of his mouth and his bushy mustache.

Like the people walking with him, Mendes had been a rubber tapper for most of his life. Like them, Mendes had spent his days collecting the milky juice that flows from the bark of the rubber tree when it is cut. The juice, known as latex, is used to make tires, sports equipment, athletic shoes, and a variety of other rubber products that people use every day.

Rubber tappers earn their living by selling a product that they take out of, or extract from, the forest. They extract latex from the rubber trees without hurting the trees or destroying the forest. This method of harvesting products without permanently harming the land is called sustainable agriculture.

But not everyone in the Amazon rain forest practices sustainable agriculture. There are many people who make their living from the destruction of the rain forest.

Cattle ranchers and farmers cut down thousands of acres of forest each year—a process called deforestation. They use the cleared land to raise cattle or grow crops. Builders plow down large tracts of the forest to construct new roads. Hardwood trees that have stood for hundreds of years are toppled every day for the lumber industry. The many rivers of the rain forest are now polluted with the chemicals used by mining companies.

The rain forest is being destroyed at an alarming rate. As the forest is cut down and burned and polluted, the abundant life within its dark green borders is also being destroyed. The plants and birds, the insects and flowers, the animals and trees of the forest—these all depend on each other and their environment.

The plants and animals that live in the rain forest form a pattern, or network, of relationships. This network of relationships among living things and their environment is called an ecosystem. Although the rain forest is huge, its ecosystem is easily endangered. Each time an area of the forest is cut down, hundreds, maybe thousands, of species of plants and animals are destroyed.

This destruction threatens more than the life of the forest. It endangers more than the livelihood of the rubber tappers. As Chico Mendes learned in his fight to save the Amazon, the destruction of the rain forest threatens the environment of the whole planet.

The fate of the planet, however, was not the main worry of the rubber tappers who walked with Mendes that hot summer day in 1986. The only way of life most of them had ever known was at stake. Chico Mendes led the group away from the deforested land. They followed a rough path that wound into the forest.

Once in the forest, they left behind the brightness of the day. They were suddenly plunged into a never-ending twilight. As the group marched on, they began to sing. Their voices rose up and were lost in the dense greenery of the trees. Along the way, they passed the log-and-grass houses of other rubber tappers. They walked on for hours.

Deep in the forest, they heard a disturbing sound—the sound of a chain saw. Someone nearby was cutting down trees. Mendes had led the group here to try to stop the chain saw crews from destroying part of the forest. This kind of peaceful protest is called an *empate*.

Chico Mendes gathered everyone together, cautioning them about what would happen. "I am sure that there will only be a few of them," Mendes said, "and that they won't react against us. But we must show that we are peaceful. I ask you not to make them nervous, not to say anything aggressive."

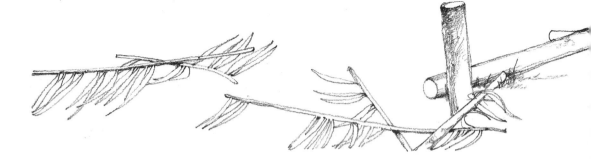

13

This protest was one of many that Mendes directed as he fought to preserve, or save, the rain forest. Mendes led this struggle not only in his home state of Acre but in all of Amazônia, the rain forest region of northwestern Brazil.

Although Mendes opposed the use of violence in his fight to save the Amazon, those who opposed him were not peaceful. In December of 1988, Chico Mendes was killed. The gentle man who had cautioned his followers to take a nonviolent approach was murdered because of his struggle to save the forest.

By the time Chico Mendes died, his struggle had gone well beyond the rain forest of South America. Because of his efforts, the fight for the forest had become a concern to everyone who cared about the environment.

"We started fighting for the rubber tree and the life we had in the forest," he said. "Then, we discovered that we were defending the whole of Amazônia."

"Now I have come to realize," Chico Mendes added, "that what we are fighting for is all of humanity."

Chapter 2

The Amazon Rain Forest

Imagine a forest so vast that it covers the land from Maine down to Florida across to New Mexico and up to Montana—and every state in between! That is the size of the Amazon rain forest, over 2.4 million square miles.

Seen from above, the Amazon rain forest looks like an endless stretch of green carpet. Actually, the Amazon is home to an incredible diversity of life. Constant hot temperatures, high humidity, and abundant rainfall create an environment in which tens of thousands of different species of plants and animals thrive.

More than 50,000 species of plants exist within the hot, wet environment of the Amazon rain forest. More than 3,000 kinds of fish inhabit the Amazon River and its tributaries. In one two-acre tract of forest, scientists discovered more than 230 species of trees. Beneath 10 square feet of decaying leaves, they found 50 types of ants. One tree alone may support more than 400 kinds of insects.

In the rain forest, violets grow 30 feet tall, and water lilies grow seven feet wide. Electric-blue butterflies flutter eight-inch wings. Beetles the size of a child's fist crawl along the dark forest floor along with caterpillars as big as snakes. There are fish, like the pirarucu, that grow to be seven feet long.

Many of these plants and animals exist nowhere else. These species depend on the unique environment of the Amazon rain forest to survive.

Located near the equator, the rain forest receives 12 hours of direct sunlight a day. The daily temperature of the forest is high (about 86° F), and a constant humidity hangs in the air. Each afternoon, drenching rains fall—more than 100 inches of rain every year.

The result of all this sunshine, warmth, humidity, and rain is the lush, green Amazon rain forest. What appears to be a carpet is actually the tops of enormous vines and trees. Their wide leaves and thick branches have grown up toward the bright sunlight to form the top layer of the rain forest, known as the canopy. The trees and plants that form the canopy reach 100 to 130 feet.

Seen closer, the canopy is more like a bumpy stretch of meadow than a flat, green carpet. The bumps are trees that, here and there, have grown up beyond the canopy. These trees are known as emergents (because they emerge from the canopy). They grow more than 160 feet above the forest floor.

The canopy contains most of the life and the color of the Amazon rain forest. It is home to many of the plants and animals of the forest.

At the top of the canopy, brilliant flowers perfume the air. Their sweet nectar attracts bees and butterflies, birds and bats. Flying from flower to flower, these forest creatures help pollinate the plants. Some of the pollinated flowers bear fruit which becomes food for the monkeys, parrots, and other animals of the forest. These animals, in turn, help to spread the seeds of the flowering plants on the jungle floor, where new plants grow.

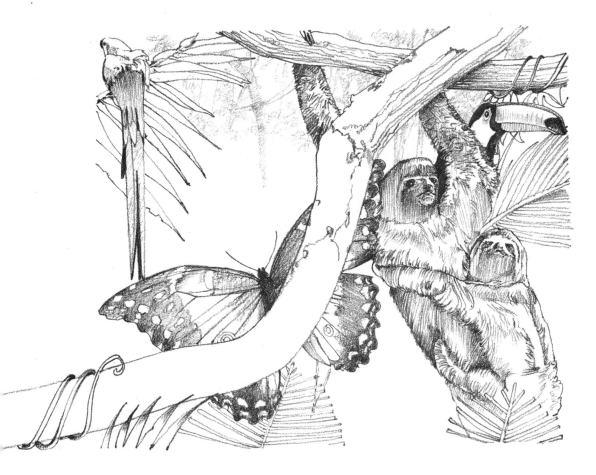

All along the canopy are brightly colored bromeliads and other types of air plants. Air plants, or epiphytes, use their roots to attach themselves to vines and tree trunks, while they get most of their nourishment and water from the air. Frogs and insects often make their forest homes in the pools of water that collect in the cup-like flowers of the bromeliads.

Beneath the canopy, 50 to 80 feet above the ground, is a second layer of plant growth known as the understory. The understory is a tangled web of bushes, woody vines called lianas, and a host of saplings and shrubs. These plants compete with each other for the scattered rays of sunshine that make it through the canopy.

The bottom layer of the rain forest is the forest floor, a spongy mat of decaying leaves and rotting logs. Direct sunlight hardly ever reaches the forest floor. It is almost clear of plant growth, except for a few small saplings.

Occasionally, one of the giant trees of the rain forest falls and opens up a space in the canopy for the sun to shine through. When the saplings are exposed to the sunlight, they shoot up toward the light, rapidly filling in the space and once more blocking the sun.

Surprisingly, the rain forest soil is thin and infertile. Centuries of drenching rains have caused the nutrients in the soil to wash away. Trees and plants have developed a shallow root system which holds the thin soil in place and prevents heavy rains from washing it away.

In the rain forest ecosystem, every creature and plant has a purpose, and nothing is wasted. Sometimes, it seems as if the rain forest is a huge recycling plant. Practically every nutrient and every drop of rain is used again and again for the benefit of the living things of the forest.

When plants die in the rain forest, they begin to decay almost immediately because of the heat and the moisture. The nutrients from decaying plants are absorbed quickly from the soil and used by other plants.

The forest also recycles most of the rain that falls on it. The immense leaves of the canopy and the branches of the understory prevent the rain from falling too rapidly to the forest floor. In fact, it can take 10 minutes before the first drop of a drenching tropical rain shower finally reaches the ground. In the intense heat and sunlight, 80 percent of the moisture is evaporated back into the air. This causes massive clouds to form over the rain forest—clouds which eventually cause more rain.

The rain forest ecosystem affects the climate of the entire earth. Huge cloud formations provide rain for the surrounding farmland. The rainfall may, in fact, cool the temperature of the earth's atmosphere. Also, the plants and trees of the rain forest absorb vast amounts of carbon dioxide from the air. (At the same time, they give off life-supporting oxygen.) The removal of carbon dioxide from the air also helps to cool the earth's temperature.

The diversity of life found in the rain forest has other benefits, too. Many rain forest plants are used as food or medicine. There may be other valuable plants that remain unknown. Scientists think that more than half of the rain forest plant species have yet to be discovered.

As vast as it is, the ecosystem of the rain forest is a fragile one. Although there are thousands of species of animals and plants in the Amazon, a single species may inhabit only an acre of the forest. When even a small area of the rain forest is destroyed, many species of animals and plants may become extinct.

When the forestland is cleared, the root systems of the trees and plants no longer hold the thin soil in place. Heavy rains quickly erode the soil, leaving behind hard and rocky land that is empty and lifeless.

24

With the forest and topsoil gone, there is nothing left to absorb the heavy rains that fall during the rainy season. Seasonal floods can then quickly destroy the centuries-old environment of the rain forest.

Scientists believe that the destruction of the forest may mean less rainfall and warmer temperatures for regions outside the Amazon. Also, burning thousands of acres of forest vegetation releases enormous amounts of carbon dioxide into the atmosphere. The release of carbon dioxide contributes to an increase in the earth's temperature. (This global warming trend is known as the greenhouse effect.)

And scientists can only guess what valuable foods and medicines may be lost when the plants and animals of the rain forest are destroyed.

The fragile ecosystem of the rain forest has emerged over hundreds of millions of years. Left to itself, the rain forest would continue to flourish. But for the last 400 years, it has not been left to itself.

Today, the ecosystem of the Amazon is threatened. Nowhere is the threat greater than in Brazil, the largest country in South America and the home of Chico Mendes.

Chapter 3

The History of the Tappers

For 10,000 years, native Indians were the only people living in Brazil. As many as 5 million Indians were spread across the country. The forest tribes lived in harmony with the land. They hunted and fished, and they gathered fruits and nuts from the forest. They also developed techniques for farming the poor rain forest soil. The Indians were part of the forest ecosystem.

In 1500, Portuguese explorers came to South America and claimed Brazil for Portugal. Settlers from Portugal brought with them their language, customs, and beliefs. The white population of Brazil grew even more rapidly in the 1690s, when thousands of Portuguese, hoping to find gold, moved to the inner regions of the country.

Portuguese settlers learned that the forest contained treasures that were easier to find and harvest than gold— treasures such as Brazil nuts, cocoa, and cinnamon. Large plantations were established for the cultivation of these crops, and the native Indians were forced to work as slaves for foreign masters. Diseases carried by settlers wiped out a great number of the Indians. So, too, did the harsh life of slavery.

Although the Portuguese settlers and the Indians were bitter enemies, the Portuguese gained an understanding of the forest from the ways of the Indians. They learned to fish and to hunt for food. They learned which plants and trees provided fruits and nuts and which ones could be used to heal wounds and cure illnesses. They learned how to collect the juice of the rubber tree and how to use it to make waterproof products.

The Indians also taught the Portuguese how to farm without harming the fragile rain forest soil. The native tribes of Brazil had been farming this way for centuries. First, they cleared a small area of the forest, being sure not to disturb any more of the forest than necessary. Then, they burned the cut trees and plants, which returned the nutrients from the plants to the soil.

The enriched soil was farmed for two or three years. But before the soil's nutrients were used up, the area was abandoned. As trees from the surrounding forest dropped their seeds, new plants and vines took over the clearing. This renewal of the forest is called reforestation.

As the foreign demand for new rubber products grew, businessmen and traders moved into the rain forest, often forcing the Indians to supply rubber for them. Then, in the late 1800s and the early 1900s, the popularity of the automobile created a tremendous demand for rubber tires. The rubber industry boomed. Deep in the Amazon, rubber traders set up large estates called *seringais*. Bosses called *seringalistas* were hired to manage the work.

Because there were no roads in the rain forest, a rubber estate, or *seringal*, was usually located near a river. The rubber was sent by boat to the markets in large cities.

To meet the increasing need for rubber, the owners of the *seringais* brought poor laborers, mostly from the eastern regions of Brazil, to the Amazon. The tappers, or *seringueiros*, came to the forest to find work, but found themselves—like the Indians—slaves to an unfair system.

The tappers were forced to buy their supplies and rent their homes from the estate bosses. Most rubber tappers owed money, therefore, before they even started to work. The tappers were not allowed to leave the *seringais* until their debts were paid. But they had to sell their rubber to the bosses, who often cheated them. By the time they paid for food, rent, and supplies, the tappers received little or no money for their hard work.

These were the conditions that existed in Acre, when Chico's grandparents arrived there in 1925. Like so many others, José and Maria Alves Mendes were looking for a better life.

Their search took them 2,000 miles down the Amazon River, but the life they found there was no better than the one they left behind. José became a rubber tapper. The family settled on the Seringal Santa Fé, where José would work for the next 20 years.

José's oldest son, Francisco, was 12 when the family came to Acre. He joined his father as a tapper. Francisco had the slim, sturdy body, dark skin, and dark eyes that were typical of the people who had migrated to Acre from northeastern Brazil. He had been born with a disabled foot and walked with a limp. Since a rubber tapper may walk many miles a day, Francisco sometimes found his work difficult. Yet he never complained and worked hard to keep up.

Francisco was a serious person. He somehow taught himself to read even though there were very few books to be found in the jungle. Chico's father enjoyed political discussions and arguments, and he would not hesitate to express his hatred of the debt system that made slaves of the rubber tappers.

In the early 1940s, Francisco married a woman named Iraci Lopes, who was tall with fair hair and bright blue eyes. On December 15, 1944, Iraci gave birth to her first child, a boy. He was named Francisco Alves Mendes Filho, but his parents called him Chico.

Chico, the oldest of seven children, was raised on the Seringal Cachoeira near the jungle town of Xapuri. The family lived in a rubber-collecting area, or *colocação*, called Bom Futuro, which is Portuguese for Good Future. They lived in the self-sufficient style of every rubber tapper in the region. (Even today, the living conditions for tappers are much the same.)

The Mendes's rubber-collecting area was about 700 acres. At the center of their *colocação* was a house and a small clearing. The house and clearing were surrounded by two or three winding rubber trails, or *estradas*.

The house, known as a *tapiri*, was a small, rectangular structure. The single-story building stood about three feet above the ground to help keep out crawling insects and animals. Sturdy stilts, made from sections of the *paxiúba* palm tree, supported the house. The wood of the *paxiúba* was also used for the walls and floors.

Paxiúba saplings were cut into slabs and used as flooring. The wood slabs were spaced far enough apart so that crumbs of bread and rice could fall through the floor. This kept the floor clean, and it also provided a tasty meal for the family's pigs, chickens, and ducks roaming around beneath the house. As in the forest, nothing in the life of the rubber tapper was wasted.

The inside of the house had a veranda, or porch, a central eating area, and several small bedrooms. Often, hammocks were hung on the porch for additional sleeping space. The roof of the house was a woven mat of two layers of palm thatch, or dried palm leaves.

The kitchen was placed off to the side so that the heat and smoke from the wood-fired clay stove did not spread through the entire house. Food was prepared and dishes were washed on a wooden platform that stuck out from the kitchen. The water that dripped off the platform to the ground became a wading puddle for the ducks and pigs below.

In the clearing, not far from the house, the family grew beans and rice, using the same farming techniques that had been taught to the Portuguese settlers by the Indians centuries earlier. They took other foods from the bounty of the surrounding forest by hunting and by gathering fruits and nuts.

As a boy, Chico spent his days like most children of rubber tappers. Childhood in the rain forest was not a carefree time. Even for very young children, the days were long and hard.

By the time Chico Mendes was five years old, there were regular chores for him to do—and little time for play. Every day, he would haul large kitchen pots brimming with water from the river to the house. Then, Chico would gather the daily supply of firewood. After that, he might have to work in the garden or prepare the freshly picked crops for dinner.

For the children of rubber tappers, childhood did not last long. When he turned nine years old, Chico was no longer responsible for fetching water or firewood. Those were the chores of the younger children. Instead, it was time for Chico to take on the responsibilities of an adult.

It was time for him to join his father in the life of a rubber tapper.

Chapter 4

The Life of a Rubber Tapper

Getting up at dawn could not have been easy for nine-year-old Chico. But life in the rain forest was not easy for young children. "My life began just like that of all rubber tappers, as a virtual slave bound to do the bidding of his master," Chico explained. "I started work when I was only nine years old, and like my father before me, instead of learning my ABCs, I learned how to extract latex from a rubber tree."

Although some of the conditions for the tappers had improved since the early 1900s, schools were still not permitted on rubber estates. "The rubber estate owners would not allow schools," Chico explained, "because if a rubber tapper's children went to school, they would learn to read, write, and add up—and then they would discover to what extent they were being cheated."

And so, each day, long before the rooster crowed to wake the rest of the family, young Chico was up. He and his father shared a breakfast of manioc (a tropical oatmeal), and thick, dark coffee. With the shadow of night still cloaking the jungle, they prepared to leave the house.

They gathered their equipment: a *faca de seringa*, the knife used to cut the rubber tree; a machete for hacking their way through any fallen trees and branches; tin cups and buckets for collecting the latex; and a large pouch for any nuts and fruit that they might find on the trails.

Francisco put on his *poronga*, or kerosene helmet. At the front of the *poronga* was a wick dipped in kerosene and positioned before a shiny disc. When Francisco lit the wick, a small flame was reflected by the disc. The *poronga* lit the way along the dusky jungle trails. (Today, rubber tappers carry modern flashlights.)

Quickly and quietly, Francisco and Chico began their work, setting out along one of the trails. The 200 rubber trees on a typical trail are spaced as much as 100 yards apart (the length of an American football field). The rubber tappers must walk at a brisk pace to reach every tree on the trail while it is still early morning, when the latex flows most freely.

Young Chico walked as fast as he could to keep up with his father. Even though Francisco limped, he moved rapidly along the rough jungle path. Chico learned to be watchful as he followed his father. There was always the danger of tripping over a fallen branch or getting tangled in one of the woody vines that snake up toward the sun. Francisco also taught Chico to keep an eye out for the poisonous snakes and insects that hide in the thick foliage of the forest.

But the most important lesson that Chico learned from his father was the same lesson taught to the Portuguese settlers by the native tribes of the forest: Francisco taught his son how to live in harmony with the forest. "I became an ecologist long before I had ever heard the word," Chico once said.

Rubber tappers must understand the delicate balance of life in the forest. Their livelihood depends on a healthy forest environment. For this reason, rubber tappers do not cut into the same rubber trees every day. Instead, each day, they work a different trail, giving the trees time to recover in between cuts. In this way, the trees stay healthy and keep on giving their milky juice.

Because their livelihood depends on the health of the forest, the tappers have a great respect for the rubber tree. Chico's cousin, Sebastião, explained the special relationship that exists between the tapper and the rubber tree. "Year in and year out, the rubber tree is like our mother," Sebastião said. "Her milk is like our blood. We go on cutting the tree, and she keeps giving milk. Every year she gives us a lot, and we go on earning our daily bread."

When he came to the first rubber tree on the trail, Francisco used his knife to make a v-shaped cut in the soft bark of the tree. Chico knew that the cut had to be at just the right depth—too deep, and it would injure the tree; too shallow, and the latex would not flow. Francisco made the cut above or below the last cut, continuing the v-shaped pattern that had been started with the first cut of the tapping season.

41

As soon as Francisco made his cut, the juice began to seep down along the v-shaped grooves. Chico placed a cup at the bottom point of the "v" mark. (If the cut were made high up on a tree, Chico would climb a homemade ladder to hang the cup.) The latex began to collect in the cup, but by that time, Chico and his father were 100 yards down the trail at the next rubber tree.

By noon, Chico and his father would have followed the looping trail back to its beginning. After a lunch of rice and beans, they returned to the forest. Retracing their steps along the same trail, and moving quickly from tree to tree, they collected the cups and buckets filled with latex juice.

Even when they returned home, the day's work was not done. The latex would have to be treated, or cured. To do this, Chico and his father would spoon the freshly collected latex onto a rod. The rod was suspended over a cone-shaped oven in which nuts and wood were burned. Layer after layer of latex was dripped onto the rod until the newly cured rubber looked like a big football.

At night, after the curing was done, Chico would climb into his father's bed. He would listen carefully as Francisco read to him. Chico wanted to learn to read and write, and his father soon realized that Chico was a quick learner.

One of Francisco's friends said, "As a kid, you'd never have thought that Chico could grow up into such a man. But he fooled you. Everyone admired how such a small kid could read so well."

By 1956, when Chico was 11 years old, he was tapping rubber full time. By then, Francisco had taught Chico all he knew about reading and counting. As Chico read on his own and his knowledge of simple addition grew, he realized that his father had taught him something else as well. Chico began to understand his father's anger about the dishonest system that kept the rubber tappers trapped in debt.

Nevertheless, like most sons of rubber tappers, Chico was likely to have spent the rest of his life tapping rubber. However, in 1962, when Chico was 17 years old, he had an experience that changed the course of his life.

It was late one afternoon, and Chico and his father were busy curing a batch of latex over a smoky fire. A stranger walked out of the jungle and began to talk with Chico's father. Although the man was dressed as a rubber tapper, he did not have the slim build of most rubber tappers, nor did he move or speak like a tapper. Even more unusual, the man carried several newspapers in his pocket—a strange sight in the Amazon. "At the time,"

Chico admitted many years later, "I didn't even know what a newspaper was."

The man, whose name was Euclides Távora, spoke about politics and current events with Chico's father. As the two men talked, Chico became intrigued by Távora's knowledge of the world outside the rain forest. Chico was impressed by how well the stranger could read. When Távora offered to help Chico improve his reading skills, the young boy sought his father's permission. By the time Távora said good-bye, Francisco had agreed to let Chico visit Távora the following Saturday afternoon.

It was a three-hour walk through the rain forest to Távora's house. But the following Saturday—and every Saturday afternoon for three years—Chico made the long trek through the forest. "He was very clever," Chico said about his new friend. "He taught me all weekend. We read the papers, and he would explain the news and tell me about the struggles of workers all over the world."

Chico and Távora also listened to radio news broadcasts, staying up the entire night to discuss world events. Távora aroused in Chico the desire to do more than just complain about the poor conditions of the rubber tappers. In one of their last conversations, Távora told Chico that the system that worked against the rubber tappers could be changed, but no one could accomplish anything alone. The tappers had to be brought together to form a strong group of workers called a labor union. "In the meantime," Chico said, "he told me to wait and to study."

In 1965, Chico's mother died during childbirth, and Chico's brother, Raimundo, who also tapped rubber, was accidentally shot and killed. Chico's father was forced to stay at home to tend the crops, which left only Chico working the rubber trails. There was no time to visit Távora, and so their friendship came to an end. Távora's influence on Chico, however, was just beginning.

"We're involved because of our ideals, and we'll never turn back."

Chapter 5

The Devastation Begins

"Without Távora," Chico Mendes felt "half lost." But Mendes began to take action on behalf of the tappers. He started to teach other *seringueiros* how to read and write. "They all wanted to learn," Mendes observed, "because then they saw how much they were being cheated."

With new confidence, Mendes sat down and wrote a letter to the president of Brazil. He complained that the rubber tappers were being cheated by the estate bosses. He explained that the children of rubber tappers were not allowed to go to school and that there were no hospitals for them when they were sick.

Mendes wrote letter after letter, but there was never a response. If he wanted to change things, Chico Mendes would have to make change happen. It would have to start on his *seringal*. So Mendes's fight for better conditions for rubber tappers started on the Seringal Cachoeira.

Mendes was impatient to unite the rubber tappers. But the tappers were used to doing things alone, and the idea of working together was difficult for them to accept. "In 1968, I tried to organize the rubber tappers," Mendes said, "and I came up against a lot of problems. It was difficult to get people interested." However, events were taking place that would soon get many people—people all over the world—interested in the rubber tappers.

In 1969, there were 30 million people living in poverty in the crowded slums of northeastern Brazil. As a solution to this problem, the government began a major effort to resettle city families. The National Integration Program was designed to move families from the eastern cities to the far western regions of Brazil—to the middle of the Amazon rain forest.

To encourage people to move, the government offered a plot of land, a two-room house, and a weekly salary to anyone who would farm the rain forest land. The government promised to build schools and hospitals for the new families and even guaranteed money to finance the cost of planting crops.

Also, the government urged ranchers to clear the forest and raise cattle. The beef could be sold to other countries, helping to bring Brazil some badly needed money.

In 1969, before the National Integration Program was announced, the Amazon was as remote as it had been when Mendes's family arrived there 35 years earlier. But from 1969 through 1975, a great deal changed. A highway, known as BR-364 (or the Trans-Amazon Highway), cut

deep into Amazônia. As work on the road progressed, giant bulldozers plowed down the forest, leaving nothing but bare earth behind. The first trees to fall were in the southern part of the Amazon. Soon, BR-364 wound its way through the jungle to Mendes's home state of Acre.

The thousands of families who traveled this road did not understand the rain forest ecosystem. As they cut and burned large areas of the forest, they did not take care, as the Indians and the rubber tappers had, to preserve the surrounding forest. As they began to farm the land, they did not know that, in a very short time, the nutrients in the soil would be gone.

When the forest soil could no longer produce enough crops for them, these settlers were forced to abandon the land and move into a new area of the forest. The land they left behind was ruined and lifeless. The land they moved to would be just as barren in a few years.

As much harm as the farmers caused, the rain forest had a much crueler enemy—the cattle ranchers. Because the soil is so poor, it takes one hectare (2.471 acres) of forest to produce enough pasture for one head of cattle. Enormous areas of the forest have to be cut and burned to create pastureland for the cattle on a large ranch.

Cattle ranchers started to attack the jungle, cutting and burning millions of forest trees. In Mendes's own town of Xapuri, from 1970 to 1975, fires and chain saw crews destroyed 180,000 rubber trees, 80,000 Brazil nut trees, and more than 1.2 million trees of other species. As the fires raged, thick clouds of smoke hovered over the Amazon rain forest.

Chico Mendes knew that time was running out for the forest and for the rubber tappers. The destruction of the forest would mean the destruction of the tappers, too. It was time for Mendes to try again to unite the tappers. "When I heard that a labor union was to be founded," Mendes recalled, "I remembered Távora's advice and went straight there, without waiting for an invitation."

Mendes joined a national workers' union in 1975, the same year that his father died. In 1976, he was elected to the town council in Xapuri. His involvement in the union and his position as councilor left him little time to tap rubber. Now Mendes was a leader of the tappers. He was like a father to his fellow tappers, standing up for them and encouraging them to stand up for themselves.

It was also in 1976 that Chico Mendes led his first protest, or *empate*. Mendes and a band of fellow rubber tappers surrounded a group of laborers who were cutting down an enormous area of the forest. The tappers kept up the *empate* for three days, until the laborers finally put down their chain saws and left the area.

The tappers and their families continued to resist the massive deforestation by the cattle ranchers. At times, as many as 300 people would come together to protect the trees. Forming a human fence, they would clasp hands and stand in front of huge bulldozers and chain saw crews. In 13 years, Mendes carried out dozens of such nonviolent blockades. It is estimated that these *empates* saved up to 3 million acres of the rain forest.

"Our movement is a peaceful one," Mendes said. "Our movement is not about spilling blood. It is a movement that tries to make the public aware of the great problems we have to confront head on."

In April of 1977, Mendes and his fellow rubber tappers formed a local labor union in Xapuri. "I got more and more involved in the labor union movement," noted Mendes. "I felt that this movement was the best place for me to participate."

As the union's influence began to grow, the ranchers decided to strike back. The peaceful protest of the rubber tappers was met with violence. Houses of union members were set on fire. Death threats were issued against union leaders and others who supported the work of the labor movement. Then, in July of 1980, Wilson Pinheiro, the union president and Mendes's close friend, was murdered.

Mendes understood that the fight to save the forest was dangerous. He saw what had happened to Pinheiro. "It could easily have been me," Mendes observed. But he also knew that the fight had to continue:

> "We're involved because of our ideals, and we'll never turn back. Our roots are too deep for us to think of giving up the struggle. They would have to kill us all to destroy the movement. I am no longer afraid of dying. I know they can't destroy us. If any of us gets killed, the movement would still go on. It might even be that much stronger."

*"Our fight is the fight of all
the peoples of the forest."*

Chapter 6

United to Save the Forest

The cattle ranchers hoped that the threat of violence would weaken the efforts of the union leaders. Instead, as Mendes predicted, the movement got stronger.

"From then on, the Xapuri rubber tappers showed the way in the fight against deforestation," Mendes said. "The Xapuri union came up with a proposal to use popular education to draw more people into the movement."

In 1979, the labor union had started a program to teach the tappers to read and write. For the first time, schools were set up for the children of the rain forest.

Then, in 1980, the union began an educational program called *Projeto Seringueiro* (the Rubber Tapper Project). Its goal, Mendes noted, was "to encourage the rubber tappers to identify more closely with the rain forest. We wanted the tappers to learn more about the forest, to understand its ways, and to be prepared to defend it."

Mendes's union work took a great toll on his personal life. His first marriage had already failed. In 1983, Mendes married a woman he had known for many years, Ilzamar Gadelha. In 1984, their daughter Elenira was born. It was often a lonely and difficult life for Ilzamar.

"Many times I was upset that Chico didn't have time for me," she remembers. "But as he explained his work to me, I began to see that it was important, and I began to understand."

As the tappers continued their struggle, they saw that they needed a plan for the forest. They needed to convince the government that it made more sense to use the rain forest for sustainable agriculture than to destroy it for large cattle ranches.

"We realized that in order to guarantee the future of the forest," Mendes said, "we had to find a way to preserve the land while at the same time developing the region's economy." He did not expect the natural resources of the Amazon to be left untouched.

But Mendes also knew that "it was important to stop the deforestation threatening the Amazon and all human life on this planet. We felt that our plan should involve preserving the forest, but it should also include a plan to develop the economy."

The Xapuri union came up with the idea for a national meeting of rubber tappers to be held in October of 1985 in Brasília, the capital of Brazil. At this meeting, the rubber tappers would make a plan for the future of the rain forest.

A committee made up of members of the unions, the Rubber Tapper Project, and other groups helped to spread the word. Posters announcing the first national meeting of the tappers were hung in the forest and surrounding towns. (The posters were designed and drawn by Hélio Melo, a rubber tapper.) Committee members traveled deep into the forest to make sure that all the tappers knew about the meeting.

ENCONTRO
NACIONAL
SERINGUEIRO
AMAZÔNIA

In mid-October of 1985, rubber tappers from across the Amazon arrived in Brasília. They had traveled for days by bus up and down the hot, dusty roads of Amazônia to get to the meeting. For many of them, this was the first time that they had ever traveled beyond their own villages and towns. "Throughout all of the history of Amazônia," Mendes said, "such an event has never occurred."

The most immediate result of the meeting was the establishment of the National Council of Rubber Tappers (*Conselho Nacional dos Seringueiros*, or CNS). The CNS was set up to give the rubber tappers a united voice. Now the tappers had a union of their own. But there were other, more long-term results of the meeting.

Once the rubber tappers were united, they began to form an alliance with the Indians of the Amazon. Despite many years of hostilities between the two groups, both the rubber tappers and the Indians understood that they shared the same fight: the fight to save the forest.

"We understand that our fight today is the same," Mendes observed. "The struggle of the Indians should be the same as the fight of the rubber tappers. We are not each other's enemies. We should fight together to defend our Amazon."

"Our fight is the fight of all the peoples of the forest," Chico Mendes proclaimed.

Working to unite the rubber tappers, Mendes learned that the government had begun programs to help protect the surviving Indians. Over the past 400 years, the native Indian population had dropped from more than 6 million to under 250,000. To protect the Indians, laws had been passed to stop the destruction and development of areas in the Amazon where native groups still lived. These areas were called reserves.

Mendes decided that a similar approach might work for the rubber tappers. The areas where tappers worked could be protected from further destruction. Since rubber tappers extracted products out of the rain forest, the union decided to call these protected areas extractive reserves.

"We thought this would be the ideal use of land for Amazônia," Mendes explained. "We rubber tappers never thought ourselves to be the owners of the land. What we want is for the state to own the land and for the rubber tappers to have a right to use it."

The union of rubber tappers was soon able to form alliances with people and groups in other countries. The fate of the rain forest was now an international issue.

All over the world, people listened to reports about the destruction of the rain forest. Every second, it was reported, an area of rain forest the size of a football field was destroyed. Every year, an area of forest the size of Washington state was deforested.

Many species of plants, trees, insects, birds, fish, and other animals—and even the native Indian tribes who have made the rain forest their home—were in danger. Scientists and environmentalists warned that destroying the rain forest would be certain to have a devastating effect on the planet.

Other countries urged Brazil to stop the destruction of the rain forest. But the economic benefit of developing the region was vital to such a desperately poor country.

The proposal to develop extractive reserves showed people that many products could be harvested from the forest without harming the rain forest ecosystem in any way. In fact, this use of the forest could be even more profitable than cattle ranching.

Over a period of 20 years, one acre of land used as cattle pasture would produce only $15.05 worth of beef products. But if the same acre of land were used for the extraction of latex, Brazil nuts, and other sustainable items, it would earn $72.79 worth of products. And the standing forest would continue to produce for generations while the cattle land would soon be lifeless.

Chico Mendes had shown the world that sustainable agriculture could help both the forest and his country's economy. As Mendes campaigned for extractive reserves, environmentalists from around the world took notice.

In March of 1987, Mendes was invited to Washington, D.C., by environmental groups in the United States. There, he spoke to senators and congressmen from around the country about his struggle to save the rain forest. Those who met Chico Mendes were impressed by the strength and determination of this humble rubber tapper from the Brazilian jungle.

That same year, the United Nations presented Chico Mendes with an award for his work on behalf of the rain forest. He also received the Better World Society Protection of the Environment Medal.

At the presentation of the Better World Society medal, Mendes addressed the audience with these simple words:

"I am a rubber tapper. My people have lived in the forest for over 130 years, using its resources without destroying it. We appeal to the American people to help us. Together, we can preserve the forest and make it productive. We can secure this immense treasure for the future of all our children."

Chico Mendes was no longer alone in his struggle to preserve the forest. "Before, people talked very little about the question of the Amazon," Mendes said. "We had an isolated struggle." Now, however, Mendes and his fellow rubber tappers were joined in their struggle by people all over the world.

In June 1988, the Seringal Cachoeira in Xapuri, where Mendes had been raised, was declared the first extractive reserve. Later that year, three more areas were declared reserves. At last, the struggle to save the rain forest was moving forward.

*"I don't want flowers at my funeral because
I know they would be taken from the forest."*

Chapter 7

The Struggle Continues

"Chico Mendes will be dead before Christmas."

In December 1988, these words were being murmured all over Acre. Mendes himself had heard them. He feared that it was just a matter of time before he was murdered.

With the success of the extractive reserves, threats and violence against union members had increased. In the late 1980s, more than a thousand rubber tappers and union workers were murdered.

Chico Mendes did not want to die. "If a messenger from heaven came down and guaranteed that my death would help to strengthen the struggle, it could be worth it," Mendes wrote in a letter shortly before his death. "But experience teaches us the opposite," he continued. "It is not with big funerals and demonstrations of support that we are going to save the rain forest. I want to live."

Chico's family, which now included a two-year-old son named Sandino, was extremely important to him. He did not want his wife and children to suffer. He did not want them to be left alone.

Yet he did not feel that he could give up the struggle. "We can't run away from this fight," Mendes insisted. "We must carry on the fight. We cannot allow the workers to go on dying."

Chico Mendes escaped at least six attempts on his life. He was forced to travel with bodyguards everywhere he went. On December 20, Mendes journeyed deep into the forest to the town of Sena Madureira, where he recruited more than 400 tappers to join the union. Although friends suggested that he stay away from Xapuri, Mendes was determined to return to his home. He wanted to spend Christmas with his family.

On the evening of December 22, 1988, Mendes finished playing a game of dominoes with his bodyguards at his home in Xapuri. Just before dinner, he decided to take a shower. The shower was located in a building away from the main house.

Out in back of the house, hidden in the thick bushes at the edge of the forest, Mendes's killers waited.

Mendes started out the back door. When he flicked on a flashlight in the darkness, it was like casting a spotlight on himself. Suddenly, a spray of bullets exploded from the blackness. Mendes staggered back into the house.

Moments later, he was dead.

The death of Chico Mendes made the headlines of newspapers throughout the world. More than a thousand people turned out for his funeral.

Drenched by a pouring rain, they walked in silence to the church. One mourner carried a portrait of Mendes attached to a large wooden cross. Politicians, filmmakers, actors, journalists, scientists, and environmentalists joined the rubber tappers in their anger and grief.

These were the people that Mendes had united in his struggle to save the forest.

"I don't want flowers at my funeral," Chico Mendes once said, "because I know that they would be taken from the forest."

But for this one occasion, Mendes's friends ignored his wishes. Lovely fresh flowers were placed on his grave.

On December 26, 1988, Darci Alves Pereira, the son of a cattle rancher, confessed to the murder of Mendes. In December of 1990, more than 200 people crowded into a tiny courtroom in Xapuri for what the Brazilian press called "the trial of the century." The 22-year-old Pereira and his father, Darly Alves da Silva, were both convicted of murdering Chico Mendes. They were sentenced to 19 years in jail.

Chico Mendes's life and death were dedicated to the preservation of the rain forest, the people of the forest, and the earth itself. "What we will not tolerate," Mendes insisted, "is the destruction of Amazônia. The Amazon's destruction is a threat to the peoples of the forest and to the entire planet. It is a threat to the whole world."

Mendes's friends and followers were greatly saddened by his death. But they were not discouraged. They did not believe that Chico's fight for the rain forest could be stopped by a bullet.

In March of 1989, 200 rubber tappers and Indians came together at a meeting that Chico Mendes had helped to plan. It was the first meeting of the Alliance of the People of the Forest. Chico's cousin, Sebastião, spoke to the group: "They murdered our colleague, thinking that they would kill our struggle. But they were wrong. Here we show our commitment to the fight that our comrade led."

The March 1989 meeting issued a "Declaration of the People of the Forest." It read:

"The people of the forest wish to see their regions preserved. This alliance embraces all efforts to protect and preserve this immense but fragile life-system, the source of our wealth and the basis of our cultures."

Today, because of Chico Mendes, people all over the world are working to save the rain forest. Articles and books about the rain forest and its ecosystem are educating people about the importance of sustainable agriculture. Many people are supporting Mendes's work by refusing to purchase products made from rain forest trees or to eat beef raised on cleared rain forest land.

At his funeral, one of Chico's many friends spoke for all of his supporters: "Chico is alive in the things that he did, the things that he stood for. Our commitment is to proceed with the fight." That commitment continues today wherever people fight to save the richness and diversity of the earth.

Glossary

bromeliad — a plant of the pineapple family that often grows as an epiphyte

canopy — the top layer of the rain forest, formed by the tops of the forest trees

colocação — a rubber-collecting area

deforestation — the process by which forest trees are cut down or burned; the permanent destruction of the forest

ecology — the study of living things in their environment

ecosystem — the network of relationships among living things and their environment

emergent — the tallest kind of tree in the rain forest (a tree that grows beyond, or emerges from, the canopy)

empate — a nonviolent protest designed to stop the destruction of the rain forest

environment — the physical world that surrounds a plant or animal

epiphyte — a rain forest plant that grows on another plant but gets nourishment elsewhere

estrada — a trail that links rubber trees

extinction — the process by which a plant or animal species ceases to exist

extractive reserve	an area of rain forest set aside for the use of rubber tappers
forest floor	the bottom layer of the rain forest
greenhouse effect	the process by which atmospheric gases trap heat and cause the earth's temperature to rise
latex	the milky white juice of the rubber tree; used to make rubber products
liana	a climbing, woody vine that grows in the rain forest
rain forest	a densely forested region found in areas of heavy rainfall near the equator
reforestation	the process by which cleared forestland is renewed
rubber tapper	a person who cuts into, or taps, the rubber tree to collect latex
seringal	a rubber-tapping estate
seringalista	a person hired to manage a rubber estate
seringueiro	a rubber tapper
sustainable agriculture	the process by which land is farmed and harvested without permanently harming the environment
understory	the middle layer of the rain forest, between the forest floor and the canopy
union	a group formed to protect the rights of workers and to promote better working conditions

Index